Warrior Within

The Mental Approach of a Champion

by Kevin Brewerton

ISBN: 0-86568-168-6
Library of Congress Catalog No.: 98-61722
Order Code No. 450

Unique Publications Inc.
4201 Vanowen Place
Burbank, California 91505

Dedication

This book is dedicated to my mother and father, Sarah and George Brewerton. To my wife, Kema, and to my children, Kolby and Kaivalya.

Thank you for the constant love and support.

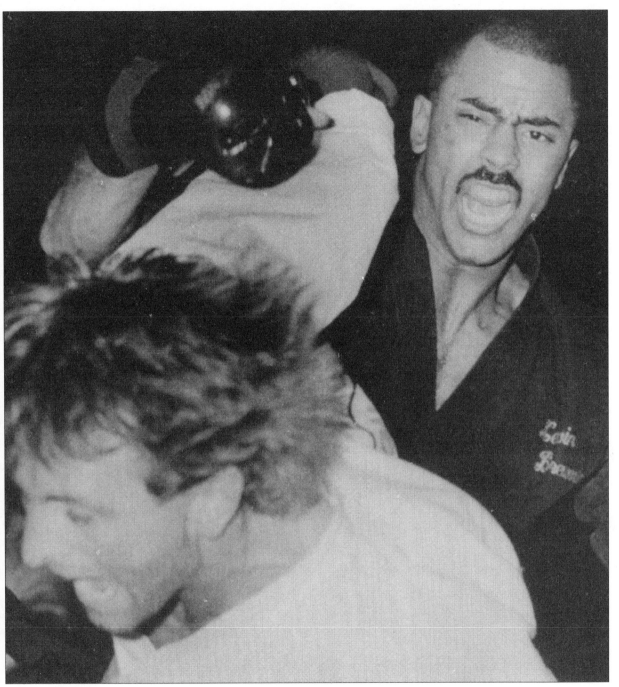

BLITZ, Birmingham 1988

Preface

by Andre Tippett

Pro footballer with the New England Patriots second round pick in 1982 NFL Draft (41st pick overall). Played in 1984-88 Pro Bowls. Named to The Sporting News NFL All-Pro Team 1985. Uechi-Ryu Karate-Do, 3rd Degree/Sandan

Kevin Brewerton's book is great reading for all martial arts enthusiasts.

Having seen Kevin compete for many successful years, I feel he has a lot to share with the karate world, especially with the new and upcoming fighters of today.

With Kevin, you are talking about a fighter who has taken a scientific approach to fighting. Along with being a quick fighter, he is a smart fighter, as seen with his international experience. I feel anyone with that type of experience and knowledge should put their ideas and thoughts into writing, to share with many. I strongly believe we can all learn and benefit from everyone, of all styles.

I am looking forward to adding Kevin's book to my martial arts library!

Acknowledgements

I would like to thank the following people that have contributed their time and effort in some way, shape or form:

Chuck Merriman
Tim Ayling
Andre Tippett
Orland Cabrera (The Mool)
Bob Fermor (Gypsy Showman)
Jerry Fontanez
Walter Bridgforth Jr
Ennio Falsoni
Archie Rullan
Alfie Lewis
Ian Weightman
Mark Byron (Cous')
Coleman
Aida Arroyo

Steve 'Nasty' Anderson
Karl Cousins (Miami)
Jos Goos
Tony Morrison
Bob Sykes
Don Rodrigues
Alain Belisle
Bjorn Olsen
Donna Wright-Bowes
Tom Festa
Kevin Cross
Paul Stewart
Paul Rayner

Photographs Courtesy: Paul Barrows, Ian Weightman, Fighters, Combat, Martial Arts Illustrated, Paul Raynor, Mark Wolwheinder, Andy Johnston

Contents

What Others Have Said

"Congratulations on the publication of your book. It is sure to be a 'must read' for any serious competitor. I know it will be a welcome addition to my dojo library. Thanks for sharing your vast international expertise with the rest of the sport karate world. It will be appreciated by all."

Chuck Merriman, 6th Dan Goju Ryu Karatedo, Transworld Oil Karate Team.

"Kevin Brewerton's name first shot to fame in 1984 when, armed solely with an ice hockey face guard, a then new style blitzing technique and a positive mental attitude, he brought a new lease on life to the UK's tournament circuit. Better known to many as 'The Jedi', Kevin's speed in movement and film star qualities were no doubt responsible for his three consecutive wins at world championship level in a sport that consists of one major drawback; that is that there aren't more fighters like Kevin Brewerton in it."

Bob Sykes, Editor-in-Chief Martial Arts Illustrated magazine

"I have had the chance to meet Kevin Brewerton in many different situations. I saw him fighting during several European and World Championships. I was a judge during one of his world title finals. I saw him teaching during his seminar in Belgium. I spoke to him many times in his spare time. I classify him, without any doubt, among the greatest fighters and the best teachers I have ever seen."

Jos Goos, President of the Belgian Kickboxing Organization

"One of the most relentless fighters I've ever encountered. Always coming after you."

Tony "Top Gun " Morrison, top ranked East Coast competitor (New York)

"Extremely impressed. One of the quickest back hands I've ever seen."

Sensei Archie Rullan, New York promoter.

"One of the fastest blitzers I've ever seen. Always putting pressure on you. Continuous puncher. And a gentleman."

Jerry Fontanez No. I ranked North American competitor (New York)

"It is my opinion Kevin Brewerton is vastly underrated. Let us not forget it was he who brought the blitz and ridgehand technique from across the Atlantic and standardized them into the British Fighters repertoire of techniques. It goes without saying that Kevin is without a doubt one of my personal and all time favorite fighters, and a worthy world champion."

Alfie Lewis 5th Degree FSKA, 4 times world champion.

"He knows all the tricks of the game, because he has such great experience. Now that he is putting his tremendous experience on paper his many opponents, fans, and new fighters will know his mental approach to fighting and learn, maybe, how to beat him one day."

Ennio Falsoni, WAKO President (Italy)

"I had the experience of fighting him a couple of times. I found him to be really aggressive. His style is really tenacious. His physical condition is always at a high level. Very fast take off from the line, he is the best fighter based in Europe there has ever been, even better than Alfie Lewis. "

Steve 'Nasty' Anderson

"Kevin Brewerton's "The Warrior Within", is a must read book for any serious Martial Artist or Athlete. Thank you Kevin for your contributions to our growth. "

Thomas A. Festa, Creator / Writer

"Kevin Brewerton's one of the smartest and most talented Sport Karate competitors of our time! "

Don Rodrigues, Team Paul Mitchell Coach

" I had the opportunity to meet Kevin for the first time at the W.A.K.O. World Championships in Atlantic City, N.J., in 1993. It was my first World Championship Tournament and I wanted to get at least one medal—it didn't matter which one. The day before the event I bought a book because I knew I would have some trouble sleeping. I was able to read half the book before I fell asleep. I have never read a book before that gave me more inspiration and taught me how to believe in myself. My mind was changed. I was here to give 100%—nothing less. On the day of the event, I gave the performance of my life. I owe it all to Kevin's book. I know the words will help others as well. Kevin is a gentleman and a Martial Artist who is willing to share his knowledge and experience with others. "

Alain Belisle, Kyokushin Style, W.A.K.O. Team Canada 1993

An Introduction

by Ian Weightman, freelance journalist and Sports Editor
of The American Newspaper

I FIRST MET Kevin Brewerton in Manchester several years ago, during a tournament on the British Freestyle Karate grand prix circuit. I had heard him on BBC Radio Four and, since my brief with The American is to write about "American sports, and Americans in sport", I arranged to interview him for a feature which appeared in the paper on May 30th, 1986.

The text of that piece, though obviously dated, still offers readers of this book with an insight into the character of its author; and I am more than happy for it to be reprinted as the introduction to his first book.

"Five-and-a-half years ago, Kevin Brewerton arrived in London, England with the intention of travelling, visiting some relatives, and most important of all, pursuing a burning ambition to one day become the best martial arts fighter in the world."

"Ever since I started in martial arts, I've always wanted to be world ranked; world rated; world class," says Brewerton, who has systematically gone about the task of proving his right to be acknowledged as the world's number one to anyone brave enough to step onto a mat with him."

"Last November he claimed the World All-Style Kick Boxing title in Budapest. And, ever since February 1985, when the British Freestyle Karate Organisation first started to keep ranking lists, Brewerton has rated as the number one fighter in the country."

"A leader in his field, 23-years-old Brewerton is nevertheless disappointed and frustrated by the lack of national recognition he has so far received."

"Victory in the World Championships in the Hungarian National Sports Centre in front of 20,000 spectators prompted one national newspaper to contact him, as well as brief interviews on Radio Four and BBC television. Brewerton, though, is adamant that it deserved more."

"Every once in a while something will go in a paper or on TV about me, and then it will snowball for a time. But it's not enough", he said. "In fact, it's real bad. If I was a world champion in any other sport, I'd get a lot more television coverage."

"Watching him in action, you tend to agree. Extrovert, charismatic and unquestionably talented, Brewerton draws crowds from far and wide to see him compete on the British Freestyle Karate grand prix circuit."

"On the mat, he is simply awesome. Away from it - like any true champion - he is still the constant centre of attention."

"The roof is on fire! The roof is on fire! Let it burn! We don't need no water!" he hollers, arms aloft and fists tightly clenched, in a theatrical demonstration of his pleasure in watching a teammate demolish a member of the opposing team."

"Alvin, you scare the hell out of me, you're so sharp," he whoops minutes later as another of his five-man team scores a three-point blow to his opponent's head."

"It is a precocious star quality, and one which causes small children to run over and shake his hand, and prompts blushing blondes to step forward to have their photographs taken with him."

"He is the first to agree, however, that without television coverage the recognition and rewards are likely to remain strictly limited. ("I'm tired of trophies ... you want some trophies?")

"I always knew I could do good. And I know that I can go to the top worldwide too, as long as I get the breaks, I want to maintain my number one ranked position here. But I also want to go to the US to compete simultaneously over there. I now want to become the first martial arts fighter to be ranked on both sides of the Atlantic at the same time."

"But there is little chance of Brewerton achieving that particular aim without the assistance of a sponsor. Presently earning a living by teaching Freestyle Karate (Kung-Fu) to classes in Farnham, Surrey; Gerrards Cross, Buckinghamshire; Fleet, Hampshire; and Greenford, Middlesex, he acknowledges, "I need a financial backer who could fly me out to the US five times a year so that I can compete on the American and British circuits."

"Brewerton won the New York Open Championship in the US last August - a competition organised by Berris Sweeney of Brooklyn, who has been visiting this country since 1983 to compete on the British circuit, and to scout for European fighters to take part in his New York promotions."

"First introduced to martial arts because his father thought it would be a good idea if he could defend himself, Brewerton turned his back on lucrative offers in other sports in which he excelled in to concentrate on becoming the best at his chosen sport.

"And while he craves for the kind of media coverage that martial arts simply cannot supply, he adds, "There is no greater reward than being the number one. I've chosen martial arts and I'm going all the way with it. They call me the best fighter of my generation."

"They" also nicknamed him "The Jedi". Something which causes Brewerton to respond in characteristic fashion; "I really don't mind what they call me, just so long as I keep on winning."

1
The Mind's Eye

A basic introduction

To be successful in tournaments of any calibre, you must possess more than mere strength and technique. It takes more than sheer power, or a good fight plan. It requires something else. Something of much greater significance. And something which is far harder than any of the other disciplines to perfect.

The mental approach of a champion is his greatest asset. It is the most formidable asset he can ever possess.

Ever since I first entered martial arts, I have always been aware that, in order to win, you require a mental edge. Yet I was almost 20 years old before I fully appreciated the fact that, in competition, it is possible that 20 percent of your performance is determined by physical ability, and 80 percent by your state of mind.

In the past, I would put so much effort into physical training, and neglect this mental approach, not knowing how to channel my mental energy. Gradually, however, I learned how to put less into physical training, and, by avoiding burn-out, devote more of my time to developing an inner sense of belief. The result has been to remove any thoughts of "I hope I can win" and, quite simply, to establish a mental edge which ensures that whenever, and wherever, I fight, I can step into the arena knowing that I can win.

By developing my inner self-belief, I found that I began to enjoy my training more. I could actually change down a gear occasionally, and still get more done. I learned there are two kinds of work: hard work, and smart work. But to be a champion, you have to be a smart, hard worker. If you achieve this, you will find that nothing is too difficult - nor is there ever a need to be in too much of a rush in preparation for a tournament. Prepare your mind, prepare you body, and you will find that there is no need to always travel in the fast lane, burning yourself out in a hasty attempt to be ready in time for the big day.

In training, or in tournaments, you must no longer think like a normal

> "Everything looks nicer when you win. The girls are prettier. The cigars taste better. The trees are greener."
>
> BILLY MARTIN, NEW YORK YANKEES MANAGER

person. Instead, you must learn to think and act like a winner.

In the simplest of terms, it is a circular process. Thinking like a winner will help you act like a winner. Acting like a winner will help make you win. Win, and you will think of yourself as a winner. And so it goes on.

But how do you actually put that circular process into motion? You have to get the ball rolling sometime - so start in your class, or in training. In our sport, most people have a mental block caused by the fear of getting hurt. But once you go out there and do some sparring, you should quickly realize it is not as bad, or as frightening, as you first thought. And that simple fact - of not getting hurt in sparring - can often start to build the foundations of your confidence.

From there, you can make progress by improving your techniques in your class and, later, by entering competitions. This is another barrier which needs to be broken. People can simply fear competition through not knowing what to expect. But confidence can be gained by entering a tournament, getting through it, and coming out of the other side unscathed, or, at the very least, intact.

The next time you enter a competition, you may do better. And eventually, you will win. Whether it is a big competition, or a small one, is unimportant. The feeling of self-satisfaction, and self worth, will be the same no matter the size of competition.

This feeling of self-worth and satisfaction is very important. But to achieve this feeling, you must be aware that when you judge yourself to begin with, this must not be done in comparison with other fighters, or you may find yourself faced with the reverse psychology of not being able to come to terms with assessing yourself alongside someone who is at a much higher level.

The next stage will be to start acting like a winner. Be free, be positive, but above all else, be decisive. There is no hiding the fact that "winners" do act differently to anyone else. They may sometimes appear arrogant, aloof and unapproachable. But mostly, it is confidence, self-belief and a passion-

19
WARRIOR WITHIN

> ## "Somebody's got to win and somebody's got to lose - and I believe in letting the other guy lose."
>
> PETE ROSE, CINCINNATI REDS

ate will to win which separates them from the rest.

To help you on your way to becoming a winner, think about what makes a punch thrown by one person in competition so very different to a punch thrown by another. Each of these punches may be thrown with just the same level of power, speed and execution as the other - yet one of them hits the target while the other is blocked, or misses. Why?

About 'attitude'

The difference is attitude. The attitude of a fighter who threw the punch and misses is: "I hope I score". The attitude of the winner is "I know I am going to score".

It all goes back to self-belief. When I throw a punch, or a kick, at an opponent I am thinking "This is going to hit him. This is going to hurt him". I even visualize the hit, just before I throw the punch. My confidence, my mental edge, gives me the energy and determination to succeed. Equally important, my opponent will also be able to sense that I am the superior fighter.

If you do not believe in yourself when you throw punches or kicks, then it will lead to you hesitating and doubting your own ability. That, too, can be sensed by your opponent.

Your self-belief will take you through any obstacle. One way of building your self-belief is to use the "reference method": where you can refer back to all-time greats who inspire you. For example, whenever I found myself under pressure, I used to - and sometimes still do - ask myself, "What would Muhammad Ali do now?" And with the great belief I have in Ali, I would visualize him bringing out the necessary skills to win. This, in turn, would give me the confidence to do the same. I would do this until my own sense of self-belief was so high that I found myself no longer needing to ask "What would Ali do now?", "What is Kevin Brewerton going to do now?" And when you get to that level, you will know your self-belief is strong enough to carry you through any challenge.

You can do the same thing by visualizing people who inspire you. It does not necessarily need to be someone from the world of boxing, or martial arts.

There are plenty of "greats" in any number of sports out there who can provide the necessary inspiration. The main thing is that it increases your confidence. And when you need additional energy - that extra edge - you will have added force in your corner.

Remember, that when you fight, your character comes through in the form of punches, kicks and motivation. A lot of people can hit hard and fast; but they do not all necessarily win. Repress your character, and you restrict your own ability.

If you are at a competition where, for some reason, you feel uncomfortable or unhappy about something, you are restricting yourself, and you will

Kevin Brewerton interviewed by Bob Pickens for the video "School of Champions"

find it much harder to maintain your technique. You will feel awkward. Nothing will go right. But if you feel free to express yourself - free of inhibitions, and not at all worried about who is watching - then your punches and kicks will be delivered with the greatest of ease. You will seem to have limitless speed and ability - mentally free and full of confidence. Hence the familiar term used by so many top athletes: "Everything just came together".

The key lies with attitude, character and the mental freedom to express yourself as an individual. Learn this and you will be able to rise to every occasion.

Similarly, awareness is a major ingredient in your training and your fighting. The powers of awareness transform confusion into knowledge and understanding. I once read a book that said, "The greatest school is life, and

> ## "The difference between ordinary and extraordinary is that little extra."
>
> ANON

the ultimate teacher is nature - but without awareness we cannot hear the teacher's call". This is very true of our everyday experiences - in, or out, of the ring.

Being aware not only helps us to recognise the mistakes we are making in the gym or competition, but also to learn about ourselves. A good fighter knows about himself: what he likes, what his strengths are; but just as importantly, what he does not like, what his weaknesses are. And he will only recognize all this through awareness.

As a competitor, we must be aware of everything that is important to us, simply to minimize our mistakes. However, awareness can also be demoralizing, as it can leave large dents in morale, as we realize that perhaps we are not quite as good as we thought we were. It's a little like shining a bright spotlight along the base of a wall, and noticing all the cracks. So be as straightforward as possible - you cannot afford to be too complex.

What motivates you?

But remember also, a hungry fighter is a winner; and to be consistent, your hunger must never be satisfied, nor your thirst quenched, until you have achieved all of your aims.

I am now the first to admit that, initially, I was a cautious fighter, as we all are to begin with. But then I saw the opportunity to become successful, and I gradually developed a hunger for that success. I would read about the great fighters of our time, and it developed in such a way that all I would ever think about was becoming one of them. Now, I have realized something else - that in order for me to stay at the top, I must always maintain that same level of hunger.

Anyone who does not possess it will not have the edge to win. Because, when the pressure is on, you will not feel there is enough to gain. It may simply be that you want to save your face, or that you do not want to be injured. So instead of being hungry for victory, you will simply back out.

Hungry fighters, however, are those who do not care about anything other than winning. They will sacrifice everything in order to succeed. They know no other way. And whether they are beginners, seasoned campaign-

Kevin and fellow competitors, Battle of Weschester, New York, 1990.

ers, or even champions, their hunger is just the same. These are the fighters who always want to win.

Look at yourself through the mind's eye to find out what motivates you, what your capabilities are, and what goals can be set.

When I first started out in martial arts, competitions were the last thing on my mind. Eventually, however, they began to assume far greater importance; and after doing reasonably well in several tournaments, I soon decided that I liked this new competitive challenge. My first goal was now beginning to take shape. Desires were beginning to take me towards ambitions.

I can recall the first tournament I went to. I looked around at the competitors in my division, and I felt totally overawed. My first goal was survival: I thought I was winning simply by staying in one piece. But then I realized that it is "anyone's" out there. Everyone has an equal opportunity to win. So why not me? Then it developed to the point where losing was no

> ## "I've tried winning. And I've tried losing. Winning's better."

PEAHEAD WALKER, FOOTBALL COACH

longer acceptable to me. I would strive to finish first.

No-one ever remembers a runner-up, no matter how good they are. When was the last time you read of a Hall of Fame full of runners-up? To make your mark in any sport, you have to be No. 1. But in saying that, you do the best you can do, and you are already a winner.

This type of attitude motivated me in such a way that sometimes I would train almost to a standstill, not knowing why I did it. I just had to. It was something inside me, pulling me towards my goal.

Call it an instinct, if you like. Winners are born and not made. Have you ever heard the expression, "He's a born winner", or, "He's a born loser"? I know that winners can be made from nothing, provided the desire is there. You can be that winner!

At first you will find yourself having to work hard to try to find some continuity in your training and level of performance. This is when your sense of awareness will be most needed - to ensure that you are training and working in the correct way. But once new demands have been met, it will become second nature. You will "just do it". The perfect fighter no longer needs to think about it consciously: it becomes instilled in his subconscious.

But don't get me wrong. I'm not saying you should not think about what you are doing. Rather, what I am saying is that once you have drilled yourself, the "computer" - your brain - will begin to work on auto-pilot. You will find yourself beginning to react on instinct.

The vital thing to take note of is that the early days of your training are the most important, since they will establish an almost unchangeable pattern, by programming your stimuli response mechanism (SRM). This mechanism is in operation from the day we are born: if a hot object is placed near to your hand, you will automatically pull your hand away. That's SRM.

We can make use of this knowledge of SRM in our own training. If we are to have SRM in our fighting, then we must be sure that the program contains the correct information. Make sure you do things right from an early stage in your training; and if you have bad habits, it is still possible to overlay the program with new information.

> "There is no such thing as second place.
> Either you're first, or you're nothing."
>
> GEORGE WEISS, NEW YORK YANKEES EXECUTIVE

Whether you establish the correct SRM from an early stage, or re-program yourself, the result will be that you will find yourself having to think less and less about what it is you are doing in training and in competition. You will be able to rely, instead, on your SRM.

We can be whatever we want to be so long as we are motivated. And just wanting to be No. 1 - a winner - is the greatest motivational force that anyone can have.

Being No. 1 is the greatest feeling I, or anyone else, can have. Being No. 1 gave me the confidence to win the World title, and to set myself new and greater goals as a champion.

Everyone has their own motivation stimuli. What works for others may not always work for you. We must learn about ourselves to become winners. Learn what makes you tick.

Eventually, training became so much easier, and I even started to enjoy the sessions. It had been hard on me. Yet today, I can say I am glad it was so tough. It set the mold, and proved to be an important motivation to do well.

Now, all kinds of things can motivate me - music, script, movies, statements, and even other sportsmen. Muhammad Ali, for example, always has, and always will, motivate me. He is a fine example of someone who is almost tailor-made for me. He trained in the famous 5th Street gym in Miami, and his flamboyant personality reflected my own natural approach to the sport.

Today, Ali's photographs still don the walls of the gymnasiums where I train - giving endless inspiration to me.

But there are all kinds of things that can help to make you "tick". People believing in you. People wanting to come up to you and shake your hand, or ask for an autograph. And it can all help to provide you with what I term as "positive thought stimuli" - the things which you should learn to store in your mind for future reference. Every time something inspirational happens to you, take that experience and store it in your memory banks. And when you need inspiration to motivate you, call it up from your

WARRIOR WITHIN

"library" of positive experiences or stimuli.

Then when you need help, either in competition, or training, you can turn to them.

Positive thought stimuli (The Library)

This is what I do when I need to step up a gear: especially when I am alone, with no-one around me for support. This is the time you most need "positive thought stimuli".

One example of this occurred at the International Grand Championships in Bermuda when I won the light heavyweight title. Although I was out there alone, I was able to motivate myself through "positive thought stimuli". Just the thought of people expecting me to win made me stronger. The thought of my students who believe that I will always win. And my father, who will be waiting for my call from the airport to let him know if I have won.

Usually, for me, the fact that I cannot bear to tell people that I have lost is often sufficient motivation for me to do well. But going into the final leg of that Bermuda competition, I found myself needing still more motivation; and by chance, I found a newspaper cutting about myself in the bottom of my sports bag, and read it to myself. All the things it said told me that I had to go out there, and to act like a winner, and the World Champion that I was reading about.

It all goes back to acting like a winner. Find out what motivates you: what makes you tick. And when you need to, use it.

On the other side of the coin, another source of energy is to think of defeats you have suffered. This will allow you to take positive stimuli from a negative experience. Our defeats can become fuel to drive us further - never allowing us to become complacent, but making us more hungry to prove, most of all to ourselves, that we can overcome any setback and reach higher levels.

Joe E. Dunn, one of the great middleweight fighters of the Jake LaMotta and Sugar Ray Robinson era once said, "The best prize of all is knowing that winning isn't always a victory, and losing isn't always a defeat." And as I've always said, defeat is a growth period - a time to learn more.

"Ninety percent of the game is in the mind."
HARLAND SVARE, FOOTBALL COACH

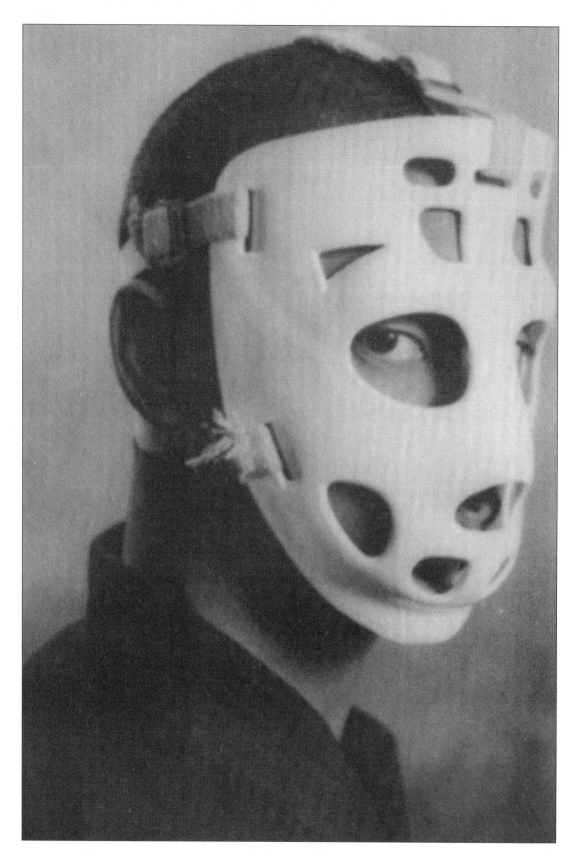

World Championships, Birmingham 1987.

Then there are the other times, when people in your corner can provide you with that added boost. Their mere presence can motivate you by giving you that added sense of security.

A glance across during a fight to see faces which say "We believe in you" can sometimes make all the difference. I know it helps me; and in return, I will do all I can for a team-mate when he is fighting. I remember standing on the sidelines once, grinding a pepper-mill whenever one of my team-mates fought. People thought I was crazy ... but to my teammate, this simply meant that it was time for him to eat his opponent.

What you shout can be important too. I know that, for me, one of the most motivating things I can ever hear is someone shouting support from my corner.

Mask of authority

It all adds up. But what you must do is to learn which methods work best for you. This will help you develop a mask of authority for your fight.

> "All things being even, the team with the mental edge will win."
>
> BILL JOHNSON, FOOTBALL COACH

We will talk more about the mask of authority in later chapters, but for the moment, it is sufficient to say that it will conceal any pain, fear or anxiety you may be feeling. It is not like a mask you wear outside to cover up what is inside - rather, it comes from inside to protect what is outside. It stems from your mind and it shows no other mental state other than one of total confidence.

That mask can be programmed to appear whenever you need it to appear. It can demoralize an opponent. You are paying the price; doing whatever needs to be done - you are always wearing the mask of authority.

It is the result of using a mental approach to your fighting.

The mind is a powerful thing, and we must learn how best to use it. Believe in yourself, and you have begun to use it already. Dig deeper into your mind, and you will increase your ability in ways that you had never thought possible.

2
Starting Out

First steps

Starting out in martial arts will be the hardest, as well as the easiest, period you will encounter in the sport. Hardest, because you are entering into a new and demanding discipline. But easiest, because, however difficult the first few classes are, you are a fresh recruit and, as such, should be rich with enthusiasm.

Enthusiasm, however, can soon diminish as progress lessens in direct proportion to the amount of time and effort that the sport demands.

This particular period is the greatest mental test for the new martial arts student, and many beginners may fall at this first hurdle.

When I first started out in martial arts, for example, I regarded it more as a novelty than a discipline.

I had done all kinds of sports at school. I was an all-rounder. I did track and field, and was real fast as a sprinter; but I did not realise that there would be many miles of running ahead of me not confined to an athletics track, but road work in preparation for an entirely different kind of competition.

I also played football and basketball; I swam a lot. I guess it all helped.

The point I am trying to make is that I am very much a natural athlete, and I recognize that I am fortunate to possess this natural ability - especially speed. But I have also recognised that no matter how naturally talented you are, there is no substitute for a consistent, disciplined training regime. Some of you who will read this will be naturally talented. Others amongst you may possess little or no natural ability at all.

For the latter, it makes no difference to the outcome, because having what it takes begins in the mind; and if you want to succeed, you will meet the challenge. There is no reason why you cannot succeed if you really want to. Yes, it will be hard at times. It was never going to be easy. But it can be done.

When I was a kid, my father suggested that it would be a good idea if I learn self-defense. I agreed, went along to a class, and really liked what I saw. It was so exciting; and I was totally overwhelmed by the atmosphere, the smell and the energy. It was electric, and I just wanted to be part of it. It became a compulsion; a sort of personal challenge, to see if I could do it.

At the same time, like thousands of other young hopefuls, I was greatly influenced by Bruce Lee. I would go to see the Bruce Lee movies. They would stimulate and inspire me. I saw "Enter The Dragon" at least 20 times when I was a kid. And each time I came out, my childhood "superhero ability" had increased that little bit more. Without probably realising it at the time, I was already being shaped.

At the very first class I attended, I did everything wrong and made the obvious mistakes. I was about 10-years-old. It all felt awkward and strange. But I was driven on by an unbelievable sense of enthusiasm, and in those few weeks, I would find myself waiting for each new class to arrive. I wanted to be good. I wanted to be able to defend myself.

I'd ride on a bus to and from school and daydream about myself fighting like some kind of superhero possessing unbelievable martial arts skills. I did not know that those early days of daydreaming had unknowingly set the wheels in motion to help me to become what I am today; because it was not simply daydreaming, but visualization - something that will be dealt with in much greater detail later in this chapter.

I had also regarded myself as a bit of a "tough guy" at school; but even my attitude began to change as I became more and more involved in martial arts. Before, I was aggressive, and would get into a little trouble. But my martial arts classes helped to change all that. I became much more disciplined, I had more control, and I was more focused.

However, after that early introduction to the martial arts, I started to find training becoming increasingly painful. The enthusiasm wore off; and after a few more months, I decided to stop.

It is a crossroads that every beginner will come to. And I reached it at an early stage, saying to myself, "This is not as much fun as I thought it would be - it's hard work!"

I started to get involved in other sports again. More importantly, I began to "hang out" with my buddies - and missed a few classes.

Soon after, however, I got into a pattern. You, too, might find that you have formed some type of structure in your training schedule - without even knowing it. Getting feedback from the rest of your class, and others in the gym, will help you, and will maintain your interest in the sport. Look at the advanced students and allow their higher level of ability to motivate you. You should even be able to find motivation by looking at

The Spoils of Glory

> "A great pleasure in life is doing what people say you cannot do."
>
> WALTER GAGEHOT

the very newest member of your class.

Something that always motivated me was the fact that my instructor always seemed to pick me out in class. He always gave me a tough time. I used to be convinced that he did not like me. To this day, I am still not sure whether he did, or didn't. But by putting me under that kind of pressure, he helped me more than he knew; and made me more determined than ever to succeed. I would put myself through a hard workout every day, so that when I was in his class he could not find any mistakes. I wanted to beat him - not in any physical sense, but on the mental plane. And in the process, what I thought was an attempt by my instructor to break me, was in fact strengthening and building my character; and, most importantly, increasing my desire to succeed.

I am not suggesting that you have to dislike your coach or instructor to succeed at this sport, because at the time, I loved mine as much as I hated him. But I am just trying to help you understand that adverse conditions can make you even stronger; and this is an important lesson on your journey to championship status.

I've always called my father "coach", because he used to always give me a hard time. If I did well, he would always say I could do better. This consequently raised my level of ability as I strived for his approval.

Physically, it was much, much tougher. But I was soon to learn that the more you put in, the more you can take out. I do not suggest that you should dedicate your whole life to any one thing. But martial arts can be a little like that; one day it is a hobby, the next it is a way of life. This is why it is important for you, as a beginner, not to burden yourself with pressures of trying to make everything perfect, or you will instantly find yourself blocking the flow of learning. It is important to you, as a beginner to find your training as enjoyable as possible. You will find it is another circular process. The more enjoyable you find it, the better you become; and the better you become, the more enjoyable you will find it.

Now, I would advise any beginners to force any thoughts of quitting out of your mind, if it is something that you genuinely want to do. It will

37

> **"If they cut my bald head open, they will find one big boxing glove. That's all I am. I live it."**
>
> MARVIN HAGLER

come. You will break that barrier.

It took me a while to make that breakthrough. It was like a picture slowly forming, which I could at least understand. Before, I was struggling to do something which I thought was martial arts. Everything was an effort. It felt like martial arts under water! But suddenly, punches and kicks which had previously felt awkward and which had taken so long to execute were feeling right. It felt good. Punches and kicks were no longer "lucky shots" - but skilled movements which could be executed with much greater ease.

It is at this moment that you will discover that your punches, kicks and techniques have some real meaning to them. Time and again, you will throw one which will feel right. You will begin to think to yourself, "Now I am doing martial arts".

This is when you will realize that it is worth pushing yourself through that barrier. You may not be a master of the sport and art, but at least you will feel that you are no longer merely practicing something without reward.

For me personally, breaking through that barrier happened one night when I was working out. It suddenly felt as if something was different - as if someone had taken my leg weights off. It was also a trememdous psychological boost. It taught me that all of the punishment was worth it. I could see that there was return for all the effort that I had been putting into my classes and workouts.

Breaking through that barrier, knowing what you want to achieve, discovering that everything has a meaning ... this will all help you with your training.

Self-motivation

One of the hardest things to establish within yourself is a sense of self-motivation. We all need a push from time to time; some more than others. But a high degree of self-motivation will make you stronger, and set you

Kevin with Chuck Merriman, 1991

aside from the average student. Working out in a club, or at a class, with fellow students and an instructor to push you along is one thing. But other days, when you are alone, with no support, with no other students around you, and with no instructor checking on you ... that is an entirely different matter.

The bottom line, quite simply, is that if you want to do something, you'll do it. But making sure that you want to do it, that is where self-motivation comes into it.

The way to look at it is like this: you are now practicing martial arts because you obviously wanted to do it. Now, let's build from there. Set yourself a program, and stick to it rigorously. But make sure it is within your capabilities. Don't ever over-reach yourself, or you will be disoriented from the start.

When I first started, for example, I used to go to my bedroom every evening at 6 pm with an alarm clock, set it for 15 minutes and work-out alone. Every evening, without missing it once.

It was a lot of hard work, but I gained mentally from that consistency. And gradually, I stretched the period of time to 20 minutes, then 30 minutes, then 45 minutes, and eventually to one hour.

It all goes back to creating the right sort of molds. It wasn't always easy, and sometimes I would look at that clock and just hope it would never reach 6 pm. But it all helped me to become self-motivated; and it helped me to set the mold.

Maybe at first, it might help you if you can arrange for a partner to join you in extra work-out sessions. You can help to motivate each other, and gradually establish some self-motivation which, in turn, will increase your inner strength. You will learn about yourself. You will learn how to push yourself, and how to get through a training session when you least want to. Then again, it is often much better to train at those times when you really do not want to. Because, if you can do it then, you will be able to do it anytime.

Very often, when my alarm goes off early in the morning, in time for me to start my roadwork session. I say to myself, "I don't feel good today. Set the clock for another 15 minutes". I may even do that, and then reset it quarter of an hour later for another 15 minutes. Sometimes, I may even start

"All things are difficult before they are easy."

JOHN NORLEY

> "When you're a winner, you're always happy. But if you're happy as a loser, you'll always be a loser."
>
> MARK (THE BIRD) FIDRYCH, DETROIT TIGERS

to think, "Take the day off. It doesn't really matter".

But that is the point when a little voice inside of me takes over and starts to say. "You can't do that. You can't lie there. Haul ass".

It is as if you are programmed. Programmed through self-motivation.

Similarly, self-motivation can help you to become a perfectionist. If something does not feel right when I am working out at the gym, then I will go over it, and over it, until I get it right. I am motivated by a feeling that I

The battle against 100 blackbelts.

want to have achieved something during a workout. I am motivated by the constant need for progress.

The progress we make is based not only on the goals we set ourselves, but also the desire we have to reach those goals. A story which I was once told, and which helps me to ensure that I never sell myself short is "The $10,000 mentality".

A new shoe salesman was given a small area in a store to sell shoes. In the first two months, he generated $10,000 worth of shoe sales. His boss was so delighted by what he saw that he gave the new salesman twice the space he originally had (to sell shoes). At the end of the next two months, his boss checked on his sales and found that he had still only sold $ 10,000 worth of shoes. Upset by this, he reduced the salesman's patch to less than half its original size. At the end of the next two months, he found that the new shoes salesman had sold $10,000 worth of shoes again.

The answer was that the salesman had $10,000 mentality.

And the lesson to be learned from this is that sometimes our mental approach to a task not only determines the goals we set ourselves, but also the level of success we enjoy.

The scale of progression

The real key to making it beyond the initial stages lies, once again, within the mind. You must set yourself a target and gradually work your way up the scale: The Scale of Progression.

Set yourself obtainable goals; and follow the four important stages of VISUALIZATION, PROGRAM, PROGRESSION, and REWARD.

How you perceive your scale of progression is important. You must remember that this scale should be designed to provide for your very own needs. If you feel that you need help on selecting your schedule from your coach, do not hesitate to ask for help, because bad habits can be hard to change.

You could, for example, always have in your mind an image of your scale of progression as being exactly like making progress up a flight of stairs. Imagine the flight of stairs as being straight and long, high and prominent. Your objective is to climb those stairs. Each week, check on your improvement: the better you get, the higher up that flight of stairs you will see yourself.

Visualization

The first step is VISUALIZATION - to have an inner vision of yourself and of what you hope to achieve in a certain period of time.

Victory over Jeff Thompson, London 1986

You may, for example, want to develop a better kick. If this is the case, then visualization is the process of seeing how you do it now, and then seeing how you want to be able to do it.

Program

Next, you set yourself a PROGRAM ... and you keep to it. With kicks, for example, this may involve 20 minutes of stretching per day, for six days a week; and for two weeks.

Progression

This, in turn, should lead to PROGRESSION - the point where you look at yourself again and check to see if there is any difference from the way that you were before you started. Inevitably, there will be some progression. Simply because you have isolated an area and worked hard with that.

If you can see that progression, then you can step up a gear, perhaps through first visualizing yourself again, then setting another program, and making further progress. And at the end of it all, you should always make sure that you give yourself some sort of reward ... maybe take a day or two off! It is simply up to you.

Martial arts is such a complex sport because there are always so many different areas which you need to develop as a competitor. As a beginner, do not make the mistake of trying to cover too many areas at once. It is always easier and quicker to develop each of the necessary skills individually, rather than try to accomplish them all at once.

You may nevertheless find it much easier to isolate different areas into groups of two to gain a maximum progression. Punching and co-ordination, for example, go hand-in-hand. As do kicking and stretching. And sparring and stamina training.

Never neglect "the scale of progression"; use it often, and use it wisely.

"When mental toughness has been rewarded by victory enough times, it adds up to the winning attitude or tradition, which is more important than coaching."

BUD WILKINSON, FOOTBALL COACH

More action from the battle against the 100 blackbelts

Even now, as a world champion, I use all four stages to help me develop into a better martial artist, and as a re-evaluation of my own development and ability.

First, I visualize which area can be developed. My own program is now set by instinct. And I will inevitably come up with better results. The key, I believe, is in using the mind; and I am at the stage now where I can obtain almost instant progression, because I have learned how best to use what ability I have. And I have capitalized upon it through self-motivation.

Reward

As for reward, I either take a couple of days off, or promise to buy myself something I have wanted if I reach the stage of progression I desire. You should also keep to a well-balanced diet throughout the week. So if you make any progression within your program, then on the seventh day of the week, you can eat what you please. The choice is yours.

But be careful. Never over-reward yourself; and always be ready to start a new program, happy with your previous progression and with the inspiration to start the next.

3
Tournament Preparation

Correct preparation

Correct preparation is essential for any fighter. Many tournaments are won days, or even weeks, before the event; and it is up to you to be perfectly tuned, both mentally and physically, at the time of the competition.

Everybody's training methods are different, but once you have discovered your own, successful way then stick with it.

When preparing for competition, the most important thing is that you build self-confidence. Create a "game-plan" which combines both mental and physical training, and if you can succeed in merging the two together, then you will find that performance is greatly improved.

That "game plan" involves working on all the areas which you feel can be improved (and it is important not to overlook any areas), and at the same time making sure that you never pull yourself down mentally.

If you tell yourself you are good, then you will feel better and perform better. Too many times, I have seen fighters criticized by their coaches for a lack of ability. If that criticism is not passed on constructively, then it can help to break your confidence, and there will be no physical improvement at all. But that really depends on you: maybe criticism, however hard to take, will help to make you more determined to prove others wrong. I hope so; or, at the very least, help you to discover the areas in need of most improvement.

The reverse of that is to tell yourself that you are good, and provided you are not complacent, it will bring results and improve performance. In a way, what you are doing is putting valuable data into the computer (your own mind).

It's a fine line, and we must be painfully realistic of our own ability. But if you are in bed on the night before a tournament, thinking about all of your negative aspects, then you will find it hard to go out there believing in yourself. If, however, at this late stage of tournament preparation, you tell yourself that you are good - even when it may not necessarily be the whole

> ## "You can't win any game unless you're ready to win."
>
> CONNIE MACK, PHILADELPHIA A'S MANAGER

truth - then you are using your mind to full advantage by programming "the computer" with positive information. Put simply, we are what we believe.

Picture your mind as a video-player. You put a cassette into it which shows that you are good; and you will enact the part that you have programmed yourself to be. Likewise, if there are any doubts in your mind, you will be bad. Remember - you cannot be what you cannot see; mold a visual through your mind's eye. It is important to surround yourself with as much positive stimuli as possible. Even when you are not aware of any change, you are being affected subconsciously. The mold is taking shape.

I sometimes hear people say "No pain, no gain". But that isn't necessarily so. Sometimes, you have got to take-out a bit of the effort you normally put into the physical side of training, and give it to the mental side. You will often get better results that way.

Competitions are long and hard, and both your mind and your body must be fully prepared. The same four stages that we used in basic training for beginners (VISUALIZATION, PROGRAM, PROGRESS and REWARD) can be used once again - only this time, the standards that are set must be that much higher, and the final goals more demanding.

VISUALIZATION is all about the competition. Usually, I visualise myself winning the competition, or doing what it would take to win the competition. This is the picture which must be maintained throughout your build-up. Not just when you are working-out, but also when you go to bed, during the day, whenever. Keep your mind working to prepare your body: the program is being set.

Visualize yourself at the competition. Use all positive aspects to your advantage. Visualize your ability against all types of opponents. See yourself driving through the opposition, eliminating them one by one - on schedule to your victory. These are the types of positive visuals that you must use to hone your ability.

People are not always aware that this is an important part of your training. Make sure that you never allow any negative thoughts to enter your

49
WARRIOR WITHIN

Kevin and Chuck Merriman

head. But if any do creep in - about a competition, or a certain type of fighter - then immediately visualize what it would be like beating that kind of fighter, and making it seem easy.

This is all helping to set the program for your fight. But at the same time, you also need a PROGRAM that you are working to. And the last thing you should do is to set yourself too-big-a-target, too-hard-a-program, and end up in pain and mentally broken to a degree where if this is the first day, what are the next two months going to be like? But be sure that no stones are left unturned and that you are thoroughly prepared.

What you must do is to start slowly and work your way up. Your strength in training must come gradually. Say, for example, if you are working over a six week schedule for a tournament, then, depending upon what shape you are in and when your last tournament was, the first two weeks should be gradual; the third week, you should increase the grade, but only

> "Achieving goals, which really means winning in some form, is the ultimate in a man's life."
>
> TOM LANDRY, FOOTBALL COACH

slightly; and now you are getting into shape, you should be able to put in two weeks of hard core training. The first week can be used to maintain the ability that you have gained - using light warm-ups, and lots of mental preparation. So that, by the time you compete, you are at your peak. As time goes by, experience will teach you how to get into peak condition and exactly how long it will take as you learn about your body and your mind.

This is a very simple exercise. What you must not do is "go over the top", or, in fight terms, you will go stale. You will reach your peak too early and there will be nothing left for the big day.

PROGRESS is measured after the tournament. After your competition, no matter how well or how badly you have performed, you can still come out a winner - provided you utilize the experience you have gained to maximum effect.

If you lose a competition, ask yourself: Why? Maybe it was a lack of punching, or bad timing. Maybe it was simply nerves. But there will always be a reason why you lost. When you have located the problem, then aim to improve it in your revised training program for progression. So at the next tournament, if you lose, it won't be for the same reason.

All along, you will be building your confidence. It will be growing alongside your experience and ability ... until you eventually win. I used to win one in 10 of my fights when I first started. Now I lose one in 50! And I could not be the champion that I am today if I had not first experienced defeat. It is a process of elimination - cutting down on error until it is finally eliminated. When two champions fight, it is usually the one that makes the fewer mistakes who will win. By concentrating on eliminating your mistakes, you will advance at a rapid rate.

Similarly, if you win a tournament, there will still be progress that can be made. Remember, you may have won a tournament, but to be a true champion, you must set your aims a little higher up the ladder, and face a higher level of opponent, until you become No. 1. Improvement can always be made. It is perfection we strive for. Fighting is a science that we must study.

REWARD is taken after a competition. Take a few days off; give yourself something you have wanted for a long time, but denied yourself the pleasure of until the job was done. If you have lost the tournament, but truly feel that there was nothing more you could have done, and that you had given it your best shot, then you should still reward yourself in some way.

But if you feel deep down that you could have done much better, and know inside that you did not fulfill your potential, then get back in the gym

"Mental toughness is essential to success."
VINCE LOMBARDI, FOOTBALL COACH

53

immediately. Work on your failings, and then take your reward if you think you deserve it.

As I have said earlier, training for a tournament should begin with plenty of time allowed for a slow build-up to the competition.

Training Schedule

Flexibility is a must for the martial arts competitor, and it is therefore important to incorporate stretching exercises into your training schedule. Good stretching will actually increase your power by strengthening your athletic posture and opening-up contracted joints. The longer the muscle fiber is, and the more flexible, the more power it has.

When you stretch, warm-up your entire body, and then isolate certain areas. Two areas to isolate are the abductor muscles, commonly known as

With son, Kolby

> ## "After the victories, you can look back at all the hard work and laugh."
>
> DON SHULA, FOOTBALL COACH

the groin; and the hamstrings. These are the major areas used for kicking.

The thing to imagine when you are stretching is your kicking ability. I visualize, as I stretch, kicks that have been improved through my stretching. I also like to visualise the good that I am doing. I like to imagine the actual muscles and see them in my own mind being stretched. I visualize kicks scored against my opponents.

Running, too, is vital - building general strength and stamina, for strengthening your feet and ankles. Vary the distance that you run. Run up hills. Run down hills. Run on straights. Run backwards. But just be prepared to RUN.

Road work is a must. There is no substitute. It is the basis from which you will build your fitness and stamina.

I use my road work as a time to visualize how I will be fighting. I find it helps to relieve some of the boredom. So I'll talk to myself. Running will target your cardiovascular system and endurance, and allow you to be more explosive in competition. And if ever I do take a break from my training or from competitions, then the first thing I do is to go for a two or three miles run.

What most people do when they wake up on a morning is to have a cup of coffee. Me - I hit the road. I roll out of bed and straight into my sneakers and then I use the first mile, or mile-and-a-half, to loosen up. I always know what sort of distance I am going to run - sometimes five miles, sometimes seven - but whatever the distance, I run alone, and I try to be mindful of how an athletics coach would treat me. That way, I never cut corners. Yet I instinctively know when I have done enough.

If, for example, I feel I have reached a peak during a training run, then I will jog the final mile-or-so to warm down. If not, then I will sprint over the last 200 metres, or more.

Sometimes, I'll sprint up hills because I find it increases my strength. And at one time, I would also use a very long street with a lot of street lamps - jogging between two of them and then sprinting between two; or jogging two and sprinting one ... or even jogging to one and then running backwards to the next one.

Skipping, as well as greatly increasing your co-ordination, can also act as a very good warm up.

When I get to the gym, for example, I will probably start by skipping non-stop for 15-20 minutes, increasing and decreasing the pace and rhythm that I skip at. I also incorporate as much footwork as I possibly can.

A clock or stopwatch can be used to improve the effectiveness of your training. For example, try skipping for 60 seconds at your regular speed, then 15 seconds as fast as you can and repeat this five or six times; then skip for 30 seconds and throw-in a 10-seconds speed run, and keep this up for 10-15 minutes; and then alternate between 15 seconds of regular-speed skipping and a 10 seconds speed-run for a further 10-15 minutes.

By now, you should be starting to feel the pace. But before you know it, you will be able to complete 30 minutes of skipping, and are fully warmed-up and ready for anything.

One final tip which helps me to enjoy my skipping, is to play music which helps sustain a rhythmic motion, as well as relieve the monotony. I use a tape with a compilation of tracks, and I change my rhythm of skipping with the music. Skipping is excellent for co-ordination, as well as hand and foot speed.

There is a great deal of discussion about how valuable weight training can be to those who practice martial arts. But I personally believe that using weights in training is worthwhile. They can strengthen you mental attitude by increasing your physical strength and power. This, in turn, will give you a sense of security and the confidence to attempt techniques which you may have otherwise not have used.

One of the main reasons why I agree with a supplementary weight schedule is that I know from my own experiences that the sport has become so much faster and harder in the last decade. There is a need to develop your body further, along with your mind. And it is not enough today to simply be a martial arts competitor - you have to be a martial arts athlete.

This book shows that you must train like an athlete. You can't be a "weekend warrior" or a "part-time fight fan" if you want to reach the top.

> "Champions are made by talent, hard work, and a little luck."
>
> TOM FLORES, FOOTBALL COACH

There is no real need to use heavy weights - use light weights to begin with and, if you feel like it, build up gradually.

In my view, applying weight training can greatly benefit your overall martial arts ability by increasing muscular density, endurance, and the reinforcement of ligaments and tendons. This results in greater punching power, strengthened stance and overall speed and agility.

I always like to combine weight training directly to my martial arts regime. However, I am constantly aware that I only utilize this form of resistance training as a supplement to my tournament preparation.

Many people have a preconception that lifting heavy weights is the only way to attain muscular size and power. On the contrary, the volume of the weight is insignificant, provided that you incorporate good form and tax your muscles with high intensity. It may be advisable to get help from someone with experience before you apply this type of training to your martial arts.

Another important area of tournament preparation is shadow boxing, which helps to develop speed and punch-kick combinations, as well as overall techniques. I prefer to use small hand weights when shadow boxing, as, I believe, this gives you even greater speed in the long run. Be careful not to use anything other than light weights here, as anything too heavy may cause ligament problems in joints.

In competition, if you can step up the pace, you can wear down an opponent; you can KO them, or slow them down considerably. You can control the fight at a comfortable and dictated pace. In the gym, however, you will be working against the clock; you can never beat it, but you can always learn to stay with it. No matter how hard, or how fast, you up your pace, in shadow boxing there is no-one that you can slow-up. You cannot have a break until the end of your time period. And all this will help to prepare you for the toughest of fights, because your body and mind will be conditioned to sustaining a high pace.

Shadow boxing is the perfect time to visualize, because shadow boxing takes the form of your imagination. When shadow boxing you, and only you, control the fight. You see it through your mind's eye.

Remember also to always shadow box for a longer period of time than you would spend fighting in competition. For two minutes in competition, do three minutes in the gym.

As you can see, visualization can be used in every aspect of your training program. I look at visualization as being the edge of a knife. It works like this: the knife represents your technique and ability - and it's your positive mental prowess which determines how sharp the blade of the knife is. With no mental imput, your knife (you) will be dull and blunt, and unable to cut. It is ineffective. It may look good, but it is useless. But with positive mental input, the edge of your knife is razor-sharp and can cut through anything.

Shadow boxing should be done in rounds. In training, I usually do six three or four minute rounds, but concentrate on just hands in the first two rounds, just kicks in the next two, and then hands and kicks for the final two. You work your own schedule to fit your needs. I'm just giving you

> "Winning is the science of being totally prepared."
>
> GEORGE H. ALLEN

some ideas.

As you shadow box, use a mirror. It will allow you to concentrate on your form and technique. And while working-out, you can watch out for any tell-tale signs of openings in your defensive guard.

A heavy bag can also be put to good effect for improving impact-power. Learn how to move the bag around with punches and kicks, but without tiring too quickly. Always make an impression on the bag by hitting it hard.

The heavy bag epitomizes gymnasiums. It is a symbol of hard work, because the heavy bag is hard work. If you use it correctly, you will improve speed, punching power, and endurance, but most of all visualization. Many of my "opponents" have taken the form of the heavy bag in my preparation for competition.

I also find it beneficial to occasionally see myself on video. I have learned that by watching myself fight. I can always pinpoint certain areas where I can improve. I then keep a mental note of this, and work on the relevant areas the next time I go to the gym to shadow box.

Also, look at your opponents' styles: you can learn a lot. Watch your rivals closely. Look for mistakes. You can exploit your opponents' weaknesses before you even step into the ring with them.

If you are able, keep all videos of yourself, and in time you will be able to look back on these to check whether you were using any techniques then that brought you some success, and which you can incorporate once again.

It is a never-ending process. Layer after layer of perfecting development. Looking after yourself thoroughly and honestly, analysing and re-analysing until you are completely happy with your technique.

In all preparation for tournaments, never forget that the most important thing in martial arts is fighting.

You must therefore ensure that sparring is incorporated as the centre point of your training schedule.

Sparring is arguably the most important element of the fighter's preparation. For no matter how fit or strong he may be, without a competent level of championship skill, and an equally high level of confidence in

> "Everyone has the will to win, but very few have the will to prepare to win."
>
> VINCE LOMBARDI

> "We fighters understand lies. What is a feint? What is a left hook off the jab? What's an opening? What's thinking one thing and doing another?"
>
> JOSE TORRES, FORMER LIGHT-HEAVYWEIGHT CHAMPION OF THE WORLD

his ability, he will be lost on the day of the tournament.

If I had to put my sparring sessions into words, then I would call them, "A hell of a great time". My sessions help to maintain and build-up my confidence. The only way that this happens is by learning to enjoy the thing you do most: fighting! There is something to learn from every sparring session.

When you spar, you can either be fresh so that you can work on techniques; or else go straight into it after stamina training - working on the theory that in competition you will not be under the same pressures as in the gym. My advice is that you use both methods. But the main thing is that when you spar, do so with plenty of imagination and variation.

Timing, perception, and strategy are the three things that a fighter must attain at all costs ... and they can only be gained through constant sparring, which brings a new dimension to your training.

When you spar, use all types of fighters: big or small, defensive or offensive, punchers or kickers, weaker or stronger, faster or slower. This variation will offer you the opportunity to be creative in the gym. It should also greatly increase your strategy that will ultimately determine what kind of game plan (strategic fight plan) you will use against different fighters.

For example, I will not fight a kicker at leg's length. I will fight him at close quarters and therefore stop him from using his most effective technique against me. I have fought against some of the fastest and best kickers in the world. But by using the right strategy I will nullify their favorite technique.

This is the strategy I refer to as the "Fish out of water theory".

The theory works like this: when a fish is in water, it is comfortable and able to function effectively because it is in its own environment. Take it out of the water, and it is instantly rendered useless and incapable. Everyone has their favorite techniques; and when given the opportunity to use them, they feel confident, comfortable, and at ease. My theory is that you must make them less effective by nullifying their most obvious technique. They should never be allowed to dictate the fighting environment where they will be able to settle into their best fighting ability. Like a fish out of water, your opponent must be taken out of his most comfortable environment. If you are successful in this strategy, you instantly dent their confidence, and put them in a mentally inferior position to yourself.

Back in the gym, meanwhile, you must always be aware that before anything can work in competition, you must increase the level of your sparring.

Immediately before a competition, for example, when I go into the gym I spar for at least five to six rounds before I do anything else, because I know the bottom line is that fighting will give me first place.

You may also have three or four different sparring partners, so that you can alternate them between three minute rounds. That way, they are fresh whereas you never take a break, knowing that you will be superior on "the day of judgement".

Never be afraid to get hit. But obviously take precautions and safety measures, such as a mouth piece, groin box, and other vital protectors. The

important thing is not to get injured before the tournament, but most of all ... remember: Enjoy your fighting.

The gym

If there is a place to work on new techniques and concepts, it is in the gym. Do not cut corners. Pay the price and you will be rewarded. And let the gym be your workshop. A workshop where you are only limited by your own imagination.

4
The Competition

Be professional

Once it is time for the competition, you should not only be at your physical peak, but also mentally prepared to a point where you are virtually programmed for success.

When you arrive at the tournament, remember that you have a full day's work ahead of you. Be professional. A professional competitor is a good competitor.

It is therefore essential that you feel confident within yourself. Arrive in plenty of time. Be sure you have rested well the night before, and also that you have eaten so that you do not need to worry about food during the day.

Food is an important component in your final preparation for a tournament. Try to eat well on the evening before the competition, and then have something light on the morning of the tournament. As soon as I arrive, for example, I know there will be no more eating until the competition is over.

The night before an event, take on as many carbohydrates as you possibly can for energy. And fluid is good on the day of the competition, as it helps to prevent dehydration and cramps.

Try to feel comfortable in your surroundings. Never allow a big event to intimidate you, nor a small one to make you complacent. Treat them all with the same professional approach. Learn how to draw strength from your environment, soak up the atmosphere.

You will naturally find yourself in a place much bigger than the club in which you work-out, and if some of the competitors around you seem much bigger than the guys you regularly spar against, and if there is so much activity going on around you that you feel engulfed, then you may start to feel intimidated. This can effect your mental state, and what you must try to do is to become part of the surroundings, the excitement and the atmosphere, learn to be as much a part of it as anyone else there; experience will eventually help. But it all stems from that sense of self-belief that you have in yourself.

> "I don't want to knock my opponent out. I want to hit him, step away, and watch him hurt. I want his heart."
>
> JOE FRAZIER

When you arrive, you must no longer view yourself as a competitor. You must learn to see yourself as **THE** competitor. By doing that, you will become far more effective. You must cancel-out all distractions, and focus, instead, on your responsibilities - your mission to win.

Similarly, while you may be psyched-up and ready for the challenge at a big tournament, a smaller competition may leave you thinking "This is not big enough for me - so there is no need to try as hard". There may be no atmosphere, not as many competitors, and simply no reason for you to be as sharp. But it is just as important that you never let these feelings get the better of you. If you are there to compete then you must give it your all. Just as much as if you were involved in a World title fight. You need to find that same tunnel vision. You need to give it 100 percent.

A mental edge

Most importantly, you should learn to develop a "mental edge" by building up confidence. Every fighter has a different way of going about this, and you have got to find out what it is that makes you tick. I have seen some fighters who never seem to get fired-up, for instance. They seem to be more effective when they are relaxed and mellow.

Personally, I like to get myself real fired-up: to get all my pistons pumping - that's when I am at my most effective.

I like to talk to as many people as possible - getting pumped-up and acting crazier by the tournament. Someone even asked a team mate of mine once if I was on drugs. But I really don't need to be. I am on a high, feeling

> "Everything a champion does must be in terms of winning."
>
> LES WOODLAND

World Championships 1987 – first title defense

invincible, and as if nothing will stop me. I simply refuse to lose. This is "the mental edge". It is a natural way for me to achieve it. But what works for me may not work for most people. So find your method - be it introverted or downright outrageous - and use it at every event.

Remember also to give yourself sufficient time to warm-up before you fight. Semi-contact point tournaments can last a long time, and it is always difficult to predict the duration of bouts. So while you should always be prepared for any length of delay, be ready to fight at any time.

The trick is to keep yourself "simmering". Be careful never to over-exert yourself mentally before you fight or you will find yourself over-psyched and not at your full potential mentally when the time comes for you to fight. Learn to relax, but at the same time, mentally strong and ready to start-up on time. Stress, fear and anxiety will fire you - or seem to; and it is important while waiting to fight that you can eliminate all of that.

The mind is like a computer, and you must program it accordingly. You must therefore tell it that you are relaxed, and that each bout is a simple elimination on schedule to a grand championship. If you can relax yourself, then you will relieve tension and pressure; and by telling yourself that you are not tired, that you are ready, and that you are prepared for any chal-

lenge, then you will be able to compete at any time.

Experience has taught me to talk with the officials and to find out approximately when my bout will take place. This gives me the freedom to walk around and get involved with other fighters and their bouts. Getting involved with other fighters allows me to use their matches as a mental warm up. It works like this: you have a team mate fighting, so get on the sidelines, especially if you are there in a coaching or supporting capacity. By coaching him, you are also coaching yourself, and sharpening your own game plan and strategy. You are in the fight without actually being in the fight. You are getting all of the fight stimuli without even committing yourself. Mentally, it is almost like a dress rehearsal. It also allows you to feel the energy of your surroundings at its fullest. And by now you should be feeling right at home.

I will stay as relaxed as possible, for as long as possible; but at the same time, I will be constantly psyching myself up. This period is important. It helps you to be involved in the tournament, and to be comfortable in the environment around you.

Final preparation

When the time finally comes to get ready to fight, then I will try to find

> ## "Being a champion is a frame of mind."
>
> MIKE TYSON

a quiet locker room or changing area, away from all disturbances. I will then strip down and begin some light warm-up exercises. I then pad-up - taking special care as I tape my hands as I am visualizing. If I am not happy with the taping, I will do it again, and again, until my hands are comfortable. This is vital for those of you that wear hand wraps. Never wear them too tight, or you will restrict the circulation and after three or four rounds, your hands will become sore and painful.

With Nasty Anderson, Bermuda grand championships

I have certain uniforms that I only use for competition, so that when I don them and tape up my hands I am intensifying my character and persona like a superhero. It is a ritual that helps my mental preparation. Basketball's Michael Jordan once shaved his head so that when his new hair grew back he would also be a new person. As you can see, there are many ways to fortify your mental strength. At the same time, I will have an inner vision of me defeating my opponent. I never pose any problems. I tell myself it will be easy. I tell myself it will be fun. I tell myself it will feel right. If it is an opponent I have fought before and they have posed some problems, then I will visualize myself beating them more easily than ever before. If I have fought them before, and beaten them easily, I will tell myself "Let's go out there and beat them again".

Something else I use to psyche myself into performances is to tell myself that I am going out there to create a masterpiece - a never forgotten work of art that will be regarded as a classic and that my performance will capture the imagination of the fight fans and competitors alike.

You see, instilling this type of positive mental attitude (PMA) will allow you to be as effective as you can be. I look at it like this: your spirit and mind is the driving force; the body is merely the vehicle that carries your creativity through movement and action.

Sometimes, I even tell myself, "Let's punish them for getting into the same ring as me. Punish them, and show them why I am No. 1. Punish them, and leave no doubts in anyone's mind."

By now, I am ready to reappear. Utterly ready and fully prepared, and ready to cause CHAOS! Some last minute hype. And from then on, anything can happen! My aim is simply to take over everyone out there. Even the referees - I won't let them deny me any points. I am out there to win.

A psychological advantage

One of the key factors in helping you to win is the psychological advantage you can establish over your opponent.

There are many ways to "psych out" your opponent and thus gain superiority over him, even before stepping into the fight zone. Glaring, laughing, warming-up in an ominous manner, can all have the effect of putting your opponent in an inferior position.

The name of the game is to win. And if you can obtain any advantage, then do it.

You will find that different opponents respond in different ways. Some may lose their nerve altogether; but others may be undeterred, or may even gain strength from your attitude. I do not bother wasting my time or energy

> "I like to feel nasty and grubby. I'm not out there to win a beauty contest. I'm out there to be mean and win, not to make friends."
>
> KIRK GIBSON, DETROIT TIGERS OUTFIELDER

with fighters who clearly cannot be intimidated. Sometimes, trying to psych-out this kind of fighter can lead to them becoming even more psyched-up. So what I will do with this kind of opponent is to play it all down.

Most importantly of all - keep your mind on the fight. Once the bout starts, you will be able to tell exactly what kind of opponent you are facing by looking them straight in the eyes.

The eyes never lie. You can detect pain, anxiety, fear, confidence. Does

Action on the national circuit

Meeting the fans

your opponent look at you before a bout? Or does he try to avoid eye-to-eye contact? These are the signs of superiority and inferiority even before the fight is started. If they stare back, then you know they will not be intimidated.

If you cannot establish that advantage over them, then simply rely upon your fighting ability.

Again, I like to establish a mark of authority on my opponents before each bout by giving them a firm slap on the shoulder. You will be surprised how well this works! But then again, I may change my strategy for a different opponent. It is the game of psych.

Seconds before a fight, touch gloves and bow, and then watch for the tell-tale signs of inferiority. These are: looking at the floor; excessive blinking; or an over friendly approach (usually meaning "please don't hurt me").

A "positive" fighter, meanwhile, will have an entirely different body language. And if they are real good, they will also be able to make it diffi-

> "It isn't bad enough to just go out and beat someone. You've got to want to annihilate them. You've got to bust them up."
>
> GEORGE H. ALLEN

cult for you to read their approach. With experience, however, you should always be able to "read" your opponent before you fight.

Self-belief is what makes the difference between a punch that will hit the target and a punch that will miss or be blocked. When I fight, I smile a lot; and even shout "Thank You" when I score points. On the surface, it may look like a guy who likes to win and fool around at the same time. Look closer, and you will see a complex, psychological plan that gives more confidence and makes winning easier.

It strengthens my character and my image, and makes the opponent's job that much harder. I am confident. I have self-belief. In simple terms, "I am a winner".

The late Cus D'Amato, a legendary boxing trainer most notable for his work with Floyd Patterson and Mike Tyson once said, "It is the mark of a great fighter when he has character plus skill. A fighter with character and skill will often rise and beat a better fighter because of this. Character is that quality upon which you can depend under pressure and other conditions."

Character is the one thing that is completely different between individuals. You can ask a hundred people to throw the same punch - it might look close or even the same, but they will all throw it in a different way. That's character.

When a champion goes behind on points, that is when he is often at his most dangerous. It is the character of the fighter and his will to win that will

> "You don't have to win 'em aesthetically. You win 'em the best you can."
>
> VINCE LOMBARDI, FOOTBALL COACH

75
WARRIOR WITHIN

force him to press back. That is the mark of a true champion; and that is character.

When you fight, you must be free to express yourself - for your own character is reflected in the way you fight. Keep it basic, but effective. Use what works, stick to what you know, and remember that scoring points - not looking pretty - is what wins fights.

If you want to be a champion, you must be prepared to stop at nothing. Be a bad loser if you have to be. There's an old saying: "Hit 'em hard. Hit 'em low ... And be friends later".

I even go to the extent sometimes of talking to my opponent when I am fighting. There is a chance that this could get you disqualified, but bending the rules a little never harmed anyone except my opponents! I talk to them when we are in a clinch, or I will pull them around and do all kinds of things that will go unnoticed to anyone other than me and, more important-ly, my opponent. Or sometimes I will even do crazy things that are apparent to everyone.

It is really back to the "fish out of water" theory again.

It has the effect of throwing an opponent off balance. Even if you can get their minds going in a different direction for a few seconds then that is long enough to exploit that temporary lack of focus. They often become angry and fight with rage rather than style, making mistakes and leaving themselves totally vulnerable.

Remember that you have that computer, and that you must use every-thing at your disposal to program it to win. Different opponents will react differently, so find their weaknesses. If they can be psyched out, made to feel inferior, or even humiliated, then do it. If not, rely solely on the things that will make you win anyway - your fighting ability.

A lot of the time you do not think about it too much. You don't analyze what you do. The only time I have ever analyzed my technique is when I started to write this book. It has helped me to understand more about the way that I win; but you should never analyze too much. A winning fighter won't question himself - once the blood is pumping and the adrenalin is flowing, you will simply find yourself doing things that you never thought

> "It's only a game when you win. When you lose, it's hell."
>
> HANK STRAM, FOOTBALL COACH

yourself capable of doing. And that is because there is something at stake: winning and losing. As well as the fear of getting hurt, fear itself will motivate you.

Fear is often the energy behind you doing your best work. Fear is a very healthy emotion for a fighter, because without fear, you can fall victim to a lack of motivation.

It is worth repeating that you must feel free to do whatever it takes to win.

I am not advising you to fight dirty - especially as I take great pride in the fact that my scientific approach to the fight game to minimize unnecessary risk. I simply do whatever it takes to win.

"The Mask of Authority"

I have written about being able to "read" an opponent's mind by looking at his eyes. Just as important, however, is to learn to conceal your own state of mind from your opponent. This is what I call "The Mask of Authority".

The mask of authority is once again a product of your own computer program. Tell yourself to deny defeat, that you will feel no pain, and that you will show no fear or anxiety. If for example, you have to fight 10 rounds against an opponent, tell yourself that for those 10 rounds, there will be no weaknesses, and that you will be the model of consistency. You can take a break once the bout is over; but until that job is done, you must be prepared to withstand any pain, and to make any sacrifices.

Never let your opponent see that you are hurt, for example, because sometimes, this is all they are waiting for. One small weakness, and they will take advantage; and worse still, take the fight.

I am prepared to bleed on the inside with pain, but show nothing on the outside. If I ever do get hurt, then I will bluff my way through by smiling. It is like a game of poker: never let your opponent know he has got the upper hand.

So wear the mask of authority: a mask that shows no weakness. The

> "It's a terrible sport, but it's a sport. The fight for survival is the sport."
> ROCKY GRAZIANO, FORMER MIDDLEWEIGHT CHAMPION OF THE WORLD

mask will allow you to be more effective. It builds an invisible force-field around you which is impregnable. It gives total concentration and total confidence. It overawes all opponents as they will be unable to infiltrate your mental defense. That is the mask of authority.

Similarly, there are certain ploys that can be used to make your opponent relax just for long enough for you to take advantage of their relaxed state of mind. This is the only time that you should remove the mask of authority. When I fight, for example, I sometimes deceive my opponent in various ways - such as putting my hands on my knees and crouching down to make my opponent think that I am tired. He may then either relax, or become over-confident and leave himself for a positive offensive counterattack. Other times, I may use facial expressions to let him think I am hurt, and take advantage of him in the same way.

Never use one method all of the time. Keep switching. Keep them guessing.

Study this chapter well. Read it. Absorb it. But to actually make it work, time and experience will help you become a seasoned professional.

5
Staying At The Top

Motivation

One of the greatest sounds that any athlete of any standard can hear is the sound of cheering crowds acknowledging his victory. But getting to the top is one thing. Once you are at the top, that is when the real work begins. For without it, the only way left to go, is down.

However, I believe that - providing he genuinely wants to - a fighter can stay at the top for as long as he likes. At this point, the champion is facing his biggest opponent: himself.

The theory is that before you reach the top, you have a challenge, a goal that drives you on until the true champion gets what he wants; but once that goal has been attained, the desire is no longer as strong, because you have made it to the top. Motivation decreases, and in some instances, totally disappears.

This is the danger point for the champion who wants to continue, but cannot find the drive that once fuelled his passion for success.

This is where motivation - or a motive - can be so crucial. If an athlete is well motivated, he will enjoy longevity as a champion. If not, his reign will be a temporary one.

As a champion, I constantly need to find new goals to motivate me: things like retaining my world title, fighting 100 black belts for charity, or being featured in magazines, national newspapers, on television and radio. Things like this stimulate my concentration, and help me to go on.

"Every time you win, you're reborn. Any time you lose, you die a little."

GEORGE H. ALLEN, FOOTBALL COACH

Kevin Brewerton and Alfie Lewis in interview after "The Clash of the Titans"

When you are No.1, it is very difficult to accept anything less. Whether at your basic level, within your own region, or nationally. Being anything less becomes difficult to accept.

We have seen the faces of winners and the faces of losers. It is such an overwhelming contrast. And when you have been with the best, or are the best, then nothing else means as much.

It is very hard to stay consistently motivated over a long period of time. And to stay at your peak mentally is far harder than to stay at your peak physically. Sometimes, you have got to learn to pace yourself, so that you do not burn yourself out.

As a champion, loss of motivation may occur through the lack of major tournaments or competitions which offer you fresh opponents and new challenges. Grand prix and national circuits are a true way of instilling motivation at a high level because you have to be consistent all year round. It can be intense but it builds character. Travelling to different cities and venues maintains your hunger to prove your ability at each event. Fighting for precious national points and forging a path on the way to becoming overall grand champion is unmistakenly motivation at its highest level, because you are under pressure and stimulated into producing some of your finest work.

If you have been successful in your school or region, or as a competitor, then you may find that the best way to maintain your motivation is to try to move up a division. One example is when competitors make the breakthrough from brown belt to black belt. Maybe you were the best in the brown belt division. Confidence was probably high; and yet suddenly, here you are faced with bigger and stronger opponents with a far wider range of techniques and, of course, experience.

Crushing the Ice, victory over Sewell, 1985

> "The highest reward for a person's toil is not what they get for it, but what they become by it."

JOHN RUSKIN

This can be demoralizing. Suddenly, you are in a position where you are no longer the best, but with the urge, nevertheless, to "stay at the top". So you will find yourself starting-over. Remember the steps and experience you gained in the lower divisions when you made the steps up, and recycle that past knowledge until you finally work your way up through the ranks of the best of the black belt division - or whatever division you step up to.

When you were below the black belt division, it was almost as if you were serving an apprenticeship. But now, in black belt competition, you are on your own, and the learning process really begins - needing full and absolute motivation.

At every level, note that it is your mental state that really matters, and will determine just how effective you will become.

Visualization

Not so long ago, for example, as I was on the highway, I did something that I had not done in a long time. That something was what most people refer to as "daydreaming". I prefer to call it "visualization". And on this particular occasion, it was almost as if I had recharged myself. I felt great and re-inspired, and I remember saying to myself: "Kevin, we're beginning to dream once again, now things can really happen".

You see, without our dreams, we are nothing. Dreams and reality co-exist. I have been a champion for as long as I can remember. It was something I had always wanted to be; and the person I am now is the molded product of many years of "visualization". It all begins from a tiny thought, from a concept; an idea of what we want, or what we want to become, in the form of a visual.

Again, during a recent trip back home, I happened to come across an old notebook which I had written when I was just 13-years-old. It read "When I grow older, I want to become a world champion". Today, more than half a lifetime later, this is what I have become.

I had forgotten all about the notebook and what I had written in it. As a child, all I ever dreamt of was being a champion, and over the years I have molded myself into the person that I am today ... which is ... "The champion I have always been".

For me, that alone provides a striking example of how crucial "visualization" - or the mind's eye - can be in terms of continued success.

Being a champion is a state of the mind. Have you ever, before or after the competition, dreamt about the event? I do all the time. This is your subconscious shaping your mental character. I refer once again to Muhammad Ali, who, before even becoming a world title contender, wrote this: " I dream I am running down Broadway - that's the main street in Louisville - and all of a sudden there's a truck coming at me. I run to the truck and I wave my arms and then I take off and then I'm flying. I go right up over the truck, and all the people are standing up and cheering and waving at me, and I wave back and I keep on flying. I dream that dream all the time."

The hungry fighter

Similarly, as a winning fighter, you must constantly be looking for new goals and new challenges to motivate yourself into the hungry fighter you once were. If you are happy as a champion and feel you have done enough, then so be it: retire, and feel good about your achievements. If not, and this chapter has raised a glimmer of a challenge in your imagination, then join me now on the final leg of our journey through the mind's eye of a champion.

The mind's eye of a champion

It is here we finally step into a completely new dimension. One that is reserved for the special few. Not just the champions, but the truly great champions who pass beyond all previous accomplishments to become legends that are never forgotten.

A true champion is not merited on one day's performance. A true champion is someone who can come up from nothing, to the heights of

"Accept the challenges so that you may feel the exhilaration of victory."

GENERAL GEORGE S. PATTON

87

championship status, to maintain consistency and to come back after defeat. That is a true champion.

To reach this level, you must be able to recycle all your past knowledge into future desires. You must be prepared to start at square one once again. Only this time, as you work your way up, you are doing it with the knowledge and experience of the past. And provided you do not lose your intensity, the rewards will be even greater than before.

When I refer to beginning again from square one, I am talking about finding new goals and challenges. We spoke of the national circuit and motivation, but when you reach the top, that motivation must be rekindled. I cannot tell you what will motivate you, because different things motivate each of us. But when I found myself at this phase I looked for motivation in the form of new challenges and different fighters. It became a thrill for me to fight in back-to-back Transatlantic tournaments. The challenge of being equally recognized on both sides of the Atlantic, and of making history as the most travelled international point fighter, provided the fuel for my motivational driving force. Winning my world titles was not enough. I had to prove my championship worth against everyone.

Coping with the pressure

At the same time, try not to get trapped by the pressures of being a champion. I believe that it takes a great deal of mental energy to reach the top; and that once you become a champion, you are under the pressures of always being expected to perform at a consistently high level. The fans, the fighters around you, and your friends will expect more from you each time you fight.

We also have an ego: I cannot think of one champion who doesn't. Ego is the reason why we take most of the challenges that we do, and the reason we got to where we are, because we have something to prove to ourselves. Ego will motivate you - but don't ever let it work against you or it can lead you to demanding more from yourself than you are sometimes able to give.

If you allow this to happen, you will merely become a relentless mech-

"There's only one thing bigger than me, and that's my ego."

DAVE PARKER, PITTSBURGH PIRATES OUTFIELDER

> "Winning is like a tightrope act. If you look down you get dizzy and you can fall. If you look straight ahead, always towards an objective you must reach, you keep going."
>
> CHUCK NOLL, FOOTBALL COACH

anism, geared to win but set for self destruction.

Remember, if you are at the top - whatever the level - you are a champion. You must fight for the right reasons as a champion. You have one thing which everyone else wants. So you can call the shots.

Once you have discovered the key to your own motivation, then you must keep it going without ever stopping to become analytical or question-

Scoring points on the national circuit

> "The only yardstick for success our society has is being a champion. No one remembers anything else."
>
> JOHN MADDEN, FOOTBALL COACH AND TELEVISION COMMENTATOR

ing yourself. Do not start asking yourself or you will feel yourself slipping off the tracks, and losing your tunnel vision by becoming too analytical.

Dispel such thoughts quickly, and put your mind to fighting, because you will realize that once you start to question everything, then you will no longer be as effective. And when you are not as effective, then your confidence and self-belief starts to slip.

I try to shake off unwanted pressure at all costs, looking at the whole thing as a game. Instead, I just go out there to have some fun.

Every tournament is important, but most times I "fake myself out", telling myself that it's no big deal - even though, in reality, I would stop at nothing to win.

The most pressure I have ever felt was during the first defense of my world title in Birmingham. I had fought in harder tournaments before and had faced tougher opponents, but this time I stood to lose something: my title. To me, all that mattered was to retain it. I felt as strongly about that, as you might feel if someone was to break into your house and steal your property.

The only way to overcome the pressure and to regain my composure on this particular occasion was not to "fake myself out", but to constantly remind myself that I was the champion, and, as such, that everyone else was inferior.

You see, it is a reversed psychological process - suddenly you find yourself confronted with the possibility of losing something, before, you had all to gain and nothing to lose. Now, you have a title you do not want to lose. This will force the level of a true champion's ability even higher. The parting of the ways between a champion, and a true champion, is now being made.

What makes a great champion? What separates a champion from a great champion? How does a champion think? What are the workings of his mind? Ask yourself that.

> "This is reaching the top. That's what we all strive for no matter what profession we are in. I feel that my life is fulfilled now."
>
> LOU BOUDREAU, FORMER CLEVELAND INDIANS SHORTSTOP ON HIS HALL OF FAME INDUCTION, 1970

He is mentally tough; positive; strong. He is not afraid to overcome adversity. In fact, in some cases, he thrives on adversity. It pushes him further than he has ever been before it brings out the best in him.

True champions can produce their greatest performances when they are under pressure - when they most need to turn it on. Anyone can do it when it is easy. But not everyone can do it when it is tough and the pressure is on. That is the true test; and that is the mark of a true champion.

The amount of time that someone can stay at the top is determined by a competitor's mental approach. A fighter can stay at the top for five, ten, or fifteen years. Or maybe just one. It is simply up to the champion's state of mind.

There are champions who come and go almost overnight. A true champion, however, is determined by his level of consistency during a long career; the domination of a decade, or a whole generation of fighters. A true champion is not only someone who can win all the time, but someone who can come back after defeat. You have to have motivating goals that will take you further along the highway of success. Your challenges become the fuel that is needed to drive yourself further and further along the highway. Each time you achieve a goal, a little more fuel is used up, so you will need to refuel again the form of another challenge. And so it goes on.

The true champions are the ones that can travel the furthest without ever completely running out of fuel. Once you have achieved your overall objective, you can travel in any direction on your highway to further success - as a champion in any field.

Everyone has their own means of coping with the pressures which might otherwise inhibit their performances. But the bottom line must always be: believe in yourself.

Hype can be an asset to your mental attitude by way of reinforcing positive mental attitude (PMA). It can increase an individual's performance to the level that it can psychologically supersede the athlete's performance beyond that of his original level. A fighter who reads about himself will want to live up to everything in print, to the point where he is raising his own self belief in, and awareness of, his own capabilities.

Ali was a master of this - he created his own hype to increase the level of his performance as well as psychologically defeating his opponents months before a title fight.

You can read things about yourself and watch fight footage and find things that will keep the edge of your knife sharp.

Something I use for example, to maintain my own motivation is a quote I heard from Joe di Maggio - a former baseball legend. When asked why he played so hard each game, he simply answered: "Because there is some kid out there that may be seeing me for the first time or the last time, and I owe him my best."

The trick is to keep it going all the time. Usually, I will succeed through superior mental approach and assertive thinking.

Believe in yourself, and you will stay at the top.

Being a champion is a special gift. You never lose championship qualities. Once you become a champion, you are a champion for life.

94

6
Conclusion

The seeds of this book were planted a very long time ago. I was asked by a fan when my book was coming out, and I jokingly replied that it was on its way.

But later, I thought "Why don't I write a book?" After all, I am a champion. People want to know what I am thinking.

So my next task was to go through the many ingredients needed to make a champion, and which of these I should focus on. I thought hard about what one factor had helped me the most. And I quickly pinpointed "The Mind".

Since then, it has taken me a long time to put this book together. Work started on it several years ago. But for one reason or another, it was delayed. There were even times when I thought it might never appear in print at all. But looking back, I am glad of the delay, because there are certain things within the book that could not have been handled so well earlier in my career.

I have matured as a champion; and writing this book has helped me to teach me more about myself. Things that were instinctive, things that came naturally, things that were controlled by my subconscious, have all been analyzed and researched.

I have also learned that the term "Champion" is another way of describing "The Best". It epitomizes "A Winner". And a winner is what we all want to be at some time in our lives.

Let's face it, we all want to win at something. No matter what we are all involved in - whether you are a lawyer, a baseball player, a sumo wrestler or a Formula One racing driver - the desire to win is the same. We all want to win. We want to win the case. We want to win the ball game. We want to win the bout. We want to win the race. We want to win the World title and become a champion.

But no matter how diverse the nature of activity might be, the one thing we all share is the will to succeed: a mental approach that will provide us with the winning formula. If you have it, then no matter what field you are involved in, you can succeed. You can take a mental attitude from your field, put it to work in any other field and you will succeed. Because the mental attitude never changes. A winner thinks like a winner, talks like a winner, and behaves like a winner in every aspect of his life.

So there we have it. A journey through the mind's eye into the mental - approach of being a champion.

This book is the embodiment of many years of hard work. I have only been able to write it because of many years of pain, sweat, tears, anger, and, of course, happiness.

I have served and earned my apprenticeship. I do like to win more than anything else. But do not be afraid to to learn from the pain of defeat. It is important to experience what it is to lose, just as it is to know what it is to win.

It is only through the backbreaking toil of training that you will learn about your weaknesses and your strengths, and ultimately about yourself and who you are. The grimacing may one day transform into the smile of success.

This book also contains numerous quotes which have been included to help capture the imagination of the reader. They help to provide a clear illustration of a winner's attitude; and while you may notice that these quotes are not all attributed to fighting champions, they are - needless to say - sporting champions who share the same "mental edge".

It is important to know that this book is not the complete workings of a winner's mental edge, or, for that matter, my own psyche. There are so many factors that I could include, and equally, other dimensions I could enter in the areas I have already discussed. But if I was to write in this manner, then I would simply find myself writing forever.

Make no mistake, however, this book will provide you with the nucleus; and I have tried to present you with a platform on which you can base your own understanding of what it takes to be a winner. The subject of an individual's mind is complex, but the matter of winning must be made simple.

I hope I have helped to strengthen your mental approach and your belief in yourself.

The key is in this book, but more so within yourself.

"Attitude Monitors Talent"

MILTON KATSELAS

Charity event presentation with Bob Sykes

A rare moment, with the
greatest Muhamad Ali

99

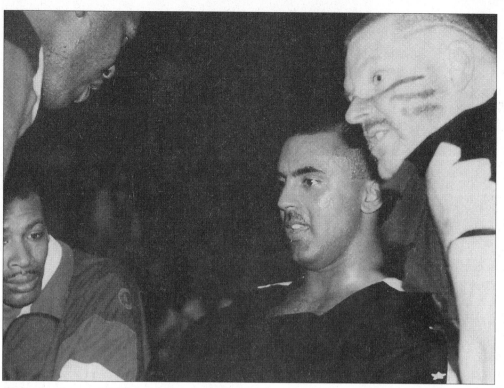

Between rounds, Birmingham 1993

Preparing for competition

Seated with Neville Wray before a 20,000 capacity crowd, Budapest, Hungary. Moments before victory the final round at the 1985 World Championships.

WARRIOR WITHIN

"Final Quote"

"Throughout the years many champions have graced our presence. Some have come and gone overnight and yet others have captured our imaginations for what seemed to be forever.

The True Champion is the one that knows no limit to his dreams and aspirations."

KEVIN BREWERTON

With Olympic javelin gold medalist Tessa Sanderson after winning first world title.

Setup stance.

Initiate lead jab offense.

Neutralize opponents shoulder with striking arm.

Follow through body punch.

Setup stance.

Block opponent.

Counter attack.

Recoil body punch.

Double up to head with the same hand.

Setup stance.

Cover and step inside opponents lead hand.

Uppercut to the body - counter.

Cross to head.

Setup stance.

Double arm block opponents round kick.

As leg descends engage counter.

Follow through cross punch.

Setup stance.

Opponent initiates round kick. Begin to move immediately to capture effective timing.

Counter with low round-kick.

Set up.

Initiate lead head thrust side kick.

Kick is blocked.

Turn into the direction of block.

Re-direct back kick, immediately capturing effective timing.

Set up.

Opponent initiates front kick.

Side step - blocking down and out.

Position counter attack.

Counter low round kick back leg.

Follow through ridge hand - or punch to head.

Opponent initiates round kick.

Immediately initiate counter movement without exposing back - while the opponent is still in chamber of kick.

Follow through back kick to body... leaving opponent no target.

Set up.

Opponent initiates kick - begin to side step while opponent is still in chambered position with kick.

Initiate lower counter block.

Set up counter attack.

Initiate hook kick.

Follow through low kick.

Set up.

Take lead arm punch.

When opponent responds - re-direct lead arm.

Follow through over the top.

Follow through to body.

Set up.

Opponent throws head punch.

Slip underneath opponents lead arm.

Counter body punch.

Follow through - Hook to head.

Set up.

Chamber kick - when opponent reacts.

Drop from chamber - redirect attack.

Lead hand to head.

Set up

Opponent initiate round kick.

Respond immediately.

Capitalize on timing front kick, counter attack.